CAPTURED
SPORTS
HISTORY

ALI'S KNOCKOUT PUNCH

HOW A PHOTOGRAPH STUNNED THE BOXING WORLD

by Michael Burgan

Content Adviser: Robert Brunette
Advisory Board Chair
Minnesota Combative Sports Commission

COMPASS POINT BOOKS
a capstone imprint

Compass Point Books are published by Capstone,
1710 Roe Crest Drive, North Mankato, Minnesota 56003
www.mycapstone.com

Editor: Catherine Neitge
Designers: Tracy Davies McCabe and Catherine Neitge
Media Researcher: Eric Gohl
Library Consultant: Kathleen Baxter
Production Specialist: Laura Manthe

Image Credits
Alamy: Peter Horree, 51, 58 (right), Pictorial Press Ltd, 17; AP Photo: 11, 19, 20, 25,
47, 48, 56 (top), Dan Grossi, 23, Harold P. Matosian, 8, John Rooney, cover, 15, 36,
37, 55, 56 (bottom), Paul Cannon, 29; Getty Images: Bettmann, 13, 21, 33, 34, 39,
43, Bob Gomel, 24, 45, George Silk, 26, 40, John Springer Collection, 9, Stringer/
Central Press, 7, 57; Newscom: dpa/picture-alliance, 5, dpa/picture-alliance/epu,
41, Everett Collection, 12, 30, Olivier Douliery, 53, 59, ZUMA Press/Allen Eyestone,
52, 58 (left); ROGERS © 2016 *Pittsburgh Post-Gazette*. Reprinted by permission of
UNIVERSAL UCLICK. All rights reserved., 54

Library of Congress Cataloging-in-Publication Data
Cataloging-in-publication information is on file with the Library of Congress.
ISBN 978-0-7565-5527-6 (library binding)
ISBN 978-0-7565-5531-3 (paperback)
ISBN 978-0-7565-5543-6 (ebook pdf)

Printed in the United State of America.
10018S17

TABLEOFCONTENTS

ChapterOne: Still the Champ 4

ChapterTwo: From Louisville to Lewiston 16

ChapterThree: Capturing the Punch 56

ChapterFour: Becoming a Legend 44

Timeline 56

Glossary 60

Additional Resources 61

Source Notes 62

Select Bibliography 63

Index 64

ChapterOne
STILL THE CHAMP

Muhammad Ali stood in the middle of the boxing ring and stared at Sonny Liston. Many called Liston "the big bear," but to Ali he was usually the "the big ugly bear." Ali was known for boasting about his skills and sometimes insulting his opponents, which had earned him the nickname "the Louisville Lip," a reference to his hometown in Kentucky. But Ali seemed to take special pleasure in taunting Liston.

At 6 feet 3 inches (190 centimeters), Ali was taller than "the big bear," though Liston outweighed him by about 10 pounds (4.5 kilograms). But Liston's reach was much longer, measuring 84 inches (213 cm) from fingertip to fingertip with his arms stretched out to the side. He could stay back from his opponent and still hit his target. (Ali's reach was 6 inches (15 cm) shorter.) Liston also had a thick chest and thighs and a powerful left-handed punch. And he could take a hard punch. In one of his bouts years before, Liston fought several rounds after Marty Marshall broke his jaw. Marshall said later that Liston "didn't even blink."

Marshall won that fight in 1954, long before Liston became the heavyweight boxing champion of the world. But Liston went almost 10 years without another loss—until a fighter named Cassius Clay beat him in February 1964 and took away his

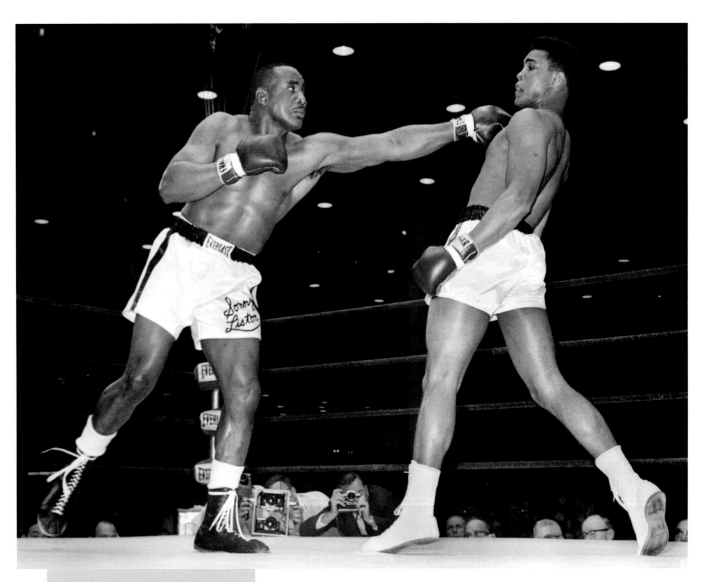

A young Cassius Clay
dodged a blow by Sonny
Liston during their bout
in February 1964.

championship. Now, more than a year later, Liston stood in the ring again for the first time since that fight, trying to win back his crown. Only now, Cassius Clay was known as Muhammad Ali, and he was determined to keep the championship he had taken from Liston.

In his first bout with Liston, Clay had been just 22 years old and had not fought anyone with as much slugging power as Liston. Clay had only boxed 19 times as a professional, though he had won each of those fights. Still, many former boxing stars and sportswriters were not impressed. When Clay signed a contract to fight Liston, former undefeated heavyweight champ Rocky Marciano said, "Clay may have the basic tools but he's at least a year away from full maturity, both physically and as a strategist." Marciano said it wasn't until his 36th fight that boxing experts "thought I knew what I was doing. Then I was like Clay is now—the talk of the town."

Despite his youth and relative lack of experience, Clay was certainly the talk of the boxing world before he stepped into the ring against Liston in 1964. He had first won national attention when he took the light-heavyweight boxing gold medal at the 1960 Rome Olympics. Unlike Liston, Clay was light on his feet, moving quickly around his opponents and throwing fast punches. He liked to say that he floated like a butterfly and stung like a bee. Some of the boxers he fought, however, were not impressed with his power. Floyd Patterson, whom Liston beat for the heavyweight title in 1962, told fellow boxer José Torres, "Clay hit me right on the chin, not once but many times. I didn't feel the damn punches. He can't punch."

Clay had won most of his fights before the 1964 bout with Liston by either a knockout or technical

He liked to say that he floated like a butterfly and stung like a bee.

Cassius Clay grabbed the light-heavyweight gold medal at the Rome Olympics; he stood with the silver medal winner (right) and two boxers who tied for the bronze.

knockout. Clay certainly had speed, some power, and the ability to avoid many of his opponents' punches. He could also talk. For years before each of his fights, Clay composed rhymes about what he would do to his opponents. Before his first fight with Liston, Clay recited a poem that said, in part: "Yes, the crowd did not dream when they laid down their money / That they would see a total eclipse of the Sonny!"

Clay ended that poem with a line that became his trademark: "I am the greatest!" Whatever shortcomings Clay had in the ring, he did not lack self-confidence. He had dreamed of becoming a

Right before his 1962 match with boxer Archie Moore, Clay predicted he would knock him out in the fourth round. And he did.

champion almost since he had first put on boxing gloves. Clay also saw the value of treating his fights as entertainment, perhaps even theater. Fans liked to root for the good guys and against the villains. They wanted to see a show. And for Clay, the show started before a match, as he shared his poems and talked trash against his foes. Some people thought "the Lip" went too far, that he bragged too much. But Clay wanted people to pay attention to his fights, and him. His outspoken style outside the ring certainly drew attention, as did his skills inside it.

LEARNING FROM GORGEOUS GEORGE

Gorgeous George took his talents to Hollywood and appeared in one movie, Alias the Champ, *in 1949.*

Muhammad Ali had a way with words before he turned pro, but in 1961 he learned that a little acting could help fill seats for a fight. He was in Las Vegas that year for his seventh fight. Before it, he met George Raymond Wagner, who was known to professional wrestling fans as Gorgeous George. He was famous for his long, blond hair. Before a match, Gorgeous George told the world what kind of beating he would give his opponent. As the two appeared on a radio show, Ali heard George say, "If this bum beats me, I'll crawl across the ring and cut my hair off. But it's not gonna happen, because I'm the greatest wrestler in the world!" At the wrestling match, Ali saw that nearly every seat in the huge arena was filled, and most of the people were yelling for George to lose. "A lot of people will pay to see someone shut your mouth," George told Ali after the fight. "So keep on bragging, keep on sassing, and always be outrageous." Ali remembered George's advice and put it to good use before the Sonny Liston fight and during the rest of his career.

Before the first fight, Clay made a point of trying to upset Liston. When they agreed in 1963 to fight, Clay said he would give Liston boxing and talking lessons, but what he really needed were "falling down lessons." He went to Liston's home in the middle of the night, honked his horn and challenged him to come out. Ferdie Pacheco, a doctor who worked with Ali for years, said, "Ali believed that the only thing that would shake up Sonny would be if he thought Ali was crazy. And that is exactly how Ali acted with him—crazy."

Clay continued this strategy until February 25, 1964, the day of the fight. The two boxers went to the weigh-in, a short ceremony for the news media that takes place before a major bout. Clay was shouting and demanding to see Liston, acting as if he were ready to fight him on the spot. He called Liston a chump and vowed, "I'm going to whup you so b-a-a-d." But underneath his tough talk, Clay had some concern. Boasting was a way for him to build his confidence. Before the fight, Pacheco saw that Clay was nervous. "This was the only time I ever really saw him nervous. The first and last time," Pacheco said later. "He was just a kid, and that night he had no idea if he could really do what he had been saying he could do all along."

Most sportswriters doubted Clay could live up to his boasts. Almost all of those who were questioned

Handlers held back an excited Clay after he was named heavyweight champion of the world.

before the fight predicted Liston would win. Some were hoping that Liston would do it convincingly, to finally shut up the Louisville Lip. But in the end, Clay did what he said he would do. He went "bear huntin'" and beat Liston for the championship. Liston said afterward that he had injured a shoulder during the fight, making it impossible for him to lift his left arm after the sixth round.

With his victory, Clay demanded respect from the reporters who had doubted him. "Never make me no

Clay won a gold-plated
championship belt
after his defeat of
Sonny Liston.

underdog," he told them after the fight. "And never
talk about who's gonna stop me. Ain't nobody gonna
stop me. Not a heavyweight in the world fast enough
to stop me. Liston's one of the most powerfulest in
the world, and he looked like a baby. I held my hands
down. I just played with him. I shook all of you up."

Clay soon confirmed rumors that had swirled
before the fight. He was converting to a branch of
Islam that had developed among African-Americans

Ali (right) and his brother, Rudy, met with Elijah Muhammad in 1964.

in the United States. Its followers belonged to the Nation of Islam, and they were commonly called Black Muslims. The founder of the group, Elijah Muhammad, soon gave Clay a new name: Muhammad Ali.

By changing his name and joining the Nation of Islam, Ali upset many white Americans. The Nation of Islam thought the black and white races should live separately, and some Black Muslims often spoke about their hatred of whites. Whatever respect Ali won for beating the favored Liston turned to anger and distrust for many people. Jimmy Cannon, a sportswriter who had never liked Clay, especially disliked him as Ali. He said Ali was using boxing as a "weapon of wickedness" because of his new religion. The World Boxing Association suspended Ali for what it called "conduct detrimental to the best interests of boxing," though several states ignored the suspension.

Finally a rematch between Ali and Liston was arranged for November 1964 in Boston, Massachusetts, but it had to be postponed when Ali became sick. A new date was set for the following May, but just a few weeks before the match, plans to use the Boston Garden fell through. The promoters quickly found a new spot for the rematch—Lewiston, Maine. So on May 25, 1965, in a high school hockey arena then called St. Dominic's, Muhammad Ali prepared to defend his title against Sonny Liston.

Several thousand people waited as the boxers stood in the ring before the fight. Lewiston, a blue-collar mill town, lacked the glamour of cities that often hosted title bouts, such as New York, Las Vegas, or Miami. Celebrities who often went to other big fights skipped this one. But some former boxing greats attended, and one of them, former heavyweight champ Jersey Joe Walcott, was serving as the referee. Just before the bout, the ring announcer introduced the boxers, and he called Ali by his new Nation of Islam name. The crowd booed.

Then a bell rang to signal the start of the fight. About halfway through the three-minute first round, Liston threw a jab that missed. He moved toward

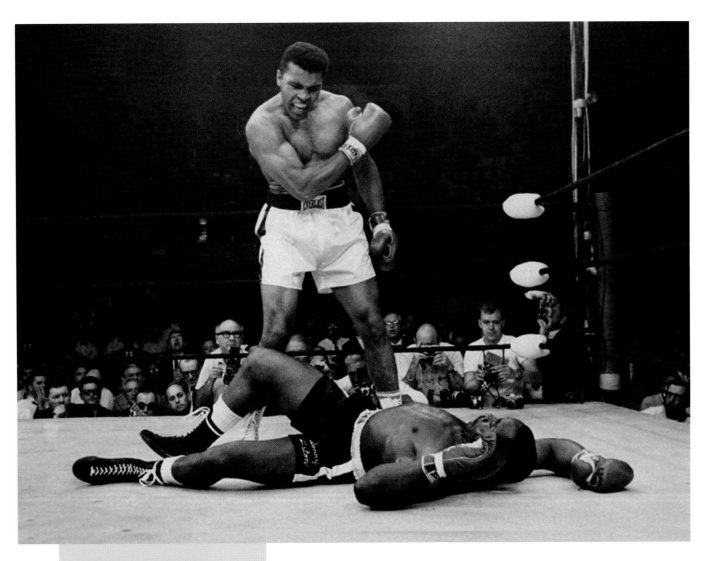

Ali stood over the fallen Liston in one of the most famous sports photos of all time.

Ali, who then threw a short, right-hand punch to the side of Liston's head. In a flash, Liston went down. Ali stood over Liston, holding his right hand as if he were ready to throw another punch. At that moment, photographers around the ring took pictures of the angry Ali standing over the fallen challenger. One of those photos became one of the most famous sports images of all time—and highlighted a controversy over the fight that still exists today.

Chapter Two

FROM LOUISVILLE TO LEWISTON

Cassius Marcellus Clay Jr. was born January 17, 1942, in Louisville, just weeks after the United States entered World War II. He learned as a boy that he might be connected to a white slave owner in Kentucky who had also been named Cassius Clay. But the earlier Clay, unlike most southern whites of the 1840s and 1850s, freed his slaves and became an abolitionist. In the Clay family of Louisville, Cassius Jr. heard that one of his great-grandfathers had lived on the white Clay's farm. On his mother Odessa's side, the boy learned, another great-grandfather had been a white Irish immigrant who married a black woman.

His father, Cassius Clay Sr., worked as a sign painter, and Odessa sometimes worked as a cook or housecleaner for wealthy white families. Together they earned enough money to buy a new house in 1946, when Cassius Jr. was 4. By then, he had a 2-year-old brother, Rudy. The Clays had more money than many black families in the city, but they faced the segregation and prejudice that were common in many parts of the United States. The elder Clay told his sons that black men could end up dead if they had a conflict with a white man. He still remembered the lynchings that had been common in the South

A young Cassius Clay kissed his mother, Odessa, in front of their Louisville, Kentucky, home; brother Rudy and father Cassius Sr. were on the porch.

when he was younger. Some of those brutal killings happened after his sons were born.

From an early age, Clay loved to talk and be the center of attention. As he said years later, "I caught on to how nearly everybody likes to watch somebody that acts different." For Clay, that meant running alongside the bus taking other kids to school, rather that riding in it. "All the kids would be waving and hollering at me, calling me nuts. It made me somebody special."

While Clay liked being somebody special, he never thought about boxing's helping him achieve that goal until he was 12. That year, someone stole his new bicycle. He talked to a white policeman who ran a nearby gym. The officer, Joe Martin, listened to the angry and tearful boy swear that he would beat up whoever stole it. Martin asked him whether he knew how to fight, and Clay said no. "You better learn to fight before you start fightin'," Martin said, suggesting that Clay come to the gym, where boxers trained five nights a week. Clay did, and he fell in love with boxing.

Martin taught Clay the basics of the sport, and in about six weeks, Clay, weighing just 89 pounds, fought his first fight. Though he still barely knew how to box, Clay won the three-round fight in a split decision. With that first win, Clay was convinced that one day he would be a champion. As time went on, he saw boxing as a good way to make money. Clay was not a great student, and he would not go to college, he thought. He later said boxing "was the fastest way for a black person to make it in this country."

Martin saw how hard Clay was willing to work to get better. The young boxer got up early in the morning to run several miles, and went to the gym after school to spar for hours. Unlike other teens, he never experimented with alcohol or tobacco. He wanted to be in the best shape possible. Despite his hard work, though, Clay developed some bad boxing habits. He kept his hands too low, instead of keeping

Clay (left) trained with another young boxer, Johnny Hampton, in 1959.

them up to protect his face. Clay counted on his fast feet and reflexes to avoid punches. But when he did get hit, Clay showed a good trait. "He wouldn't get mad and wade in, the way some boys do," Martin recalled. "He'd take a good punch and then he'd go right back to boxing, box his way out of it, the way I taught him."

During his boxing career in Louisville, Clay was already taunting other boxers. And he wrote his first poems predicting the outcomes of his fights. Before one bout, he told a reporter, "This guy must be done. / I'll stop him in one." The people around him who knew boxing could see his talent. A boxing coach told Odessa Clay that her son "must be from outer space, because I've never seen anyone like him in my life."

By the time Clay was 18, he had won several national amateur boxing championships while fighting as a light heavyweight. That year, he turned his sights to the 1960 Olympic Games in Rome.

Clay's family was at the airport to greet him when he arrived home from the 1960 Olympics in Rome.

Clay made the U.S. boxing team, but he almost didn't go to Rome because he was afraid of flying. Martin finally persuaded him to go, saying that if Clay wanted to be the world heavyweight champion someday, he needed to fight in the Olympics. Clay agreed and went on to win the gold medal.

Returning to the United States, Clay was already thinking about fighting Floyd Patterson, who was then the world heavyweight champion. Clay received some national media attention when he turned pro, and by the summer of 1961 some of his fights were being shown on TV across the country. People liked Clay—he was funny, handsome, and skilled.

While some boxing experts questioned how well he would do as a pro, no one doubted that he was entertaining. A group of white businessmen in Louisville supported his career. They paid Clay a salary and took half of the money he made from his fights. Unlike some boxers of the day—including Sonny Liston—Clay was not connected to mobsters. These organized crime members were known to influence boxing by trying to fix fights—arranging in advance who would win. By doing so, they could make money on bets for or against certain fighters. Boxers at the time were often managed by people connected to mobsters. The fighters didn't always receive their fair share of their winnings, and they risked being hurt—or killed—if they refused to do what the mobsters wanted.

Clay's Louisville backers arranged for him to work with Angelo Dundee, a respected boxing trainer based in Miami Beach, Florida. Dundee liked his new boxer. "All he wanted to do was train and fight, train and fight," Dundee said. He did not try to stop the Louisville Lip's brash talk. He just wanted to make Clay a better boxer and make sure he had a successful career. For his early fights, Dundee chose opponents he thought Clay could defeat. The strategy helped strengthen Clay's reputation. Finally, in 1963, he began preparing to fight Sonny Liston.

Cassius Clay had focused on boxing starting at
age 12. Charles "Sonny" Liston had never picked
up a glove until after several hard years on the

streets. Liston never learned to read or write, and while living in St. Louis in 1950, he was arrested. He pleaded guilty to armed robbery, and while in prison he learned to box. In his first pro bout, in 1953, he knocked out his opponent with the first punch he threw. His reputation as a devastating puncher grew. But Liston was one of the boxers who worked for mobsters. At times, the criminals sent him to beat up people who owed them money. The mobster ties, Liston's prison record, and his reputation for meanness made him unpopular in the boxing

world. But when he faced Floyd Patterson for the championship in 1962, boxing experts agreed that the bigger and stronger Liston would win.

As a boy, Patterson had spent time in a school for emotionally disturbed boys, where he learned to read and write. He started boxing at 14 and just three years later won an Olympic gold medal as a middleweight. In 1956 he won the world heavyweight championship. He lost the title in 1959 but won it back in the next year—the first time a heavyweight boxer had regained a championship after losing it.

Liston (right) bested Patterson in less than 2 minutes to win the heavyweight title in 1962.

Patterson, *The New York Times* said after he died in 2006, was "a good guy in the bad world of boxing."

Sonny Liston knew that boxing fans expected there to be good guys and bad guys in boxing, as in a cowboy movie. At a boxing match, he once said, people pay "to see the bad guy get beat." But with the Liston-Patterson fight in 1962 and their rematch after Liston won the title, people talked about another way of looking at good versus bad. Patterson represented the "good" African-American, who didn't cause trouble. Liston was the "bad" African-American

> **The racial—and sometimes racist—aspect of boxing was hard to miss.**

with a prison record and ties to crime. His image scared some whites.

The racial—and sometimes racist—aspect of boxing was hard to miss. When slavery was legal, slave owners sometimes organized boxing matches among their male slaves. Owners often bet on the matches. A former slave who turned abolitionist, Frederick Douglass, said the owners used the sport as way to keep the enslaved men from thinking about rebelling. By the 1960s, many of the best pro boxers were African-Americans. The men who ran the sport, however, were mostly white gangsters or businessmen with money. They encouraged fans—many of whom were white—to come watch two black fighters beat each other up. The fans were eager to support a "good" African-American like Patterson in his battles against Liston.

By 1963, some black writers were holding Cassius Clay up as an example for other blacks. When he said, "I am the greatest," he was talking about a self-confidence and pride that the writers thought blacks needed to show all the time. This sense of pride came as African-Americans were fighting against racial segregation and for their civil rights. Clay was not active in the civil rights movement, though he personally had experienced racism and prejudice. He knew he would not be served in certain restaurants, and a store clerk in Miami once told him to put down a shirt he had picked up. The store did not let blacks touch its clothing. For Clay, the solution was to make money as a boxer. Then he could live the way he wanted. He surprised some people when he said he didn't support racial integration. He had no use for the National Association for the Advancement of Colored People (NAACP), which was trying to use legal, peaceful means to help blacks win their rights. "I'm a fighter," Clay said. "I believe in the eye-for-an-eye business. I'm no cheek-turner."

Some of Clay's ideas about race came from his interest in the Nation of Islam. In 1962 he became friends with Malcolm X, a prominent member of the organization. Malcolm stressed the idea that blacks and whites should not live side by side. He once said God had killed 120 whites in a plane crash as an answer to the Black Muslims' prayers. Even before meeting Malcolm, Clay had heard Nation of Islam speakers. They talked about the slavery that had built much of the United States and about continuing racism. For Clay, the ideas seemed to go with the stories his father had told him about lynchings and racism. And he was impressed with Malcolm X's speaking ability. "He was fearless," Clay later said. "That really attracted me."

Clay tried to keep his interest in the Nation of Islam a secret. For three years, he later said, "I'd sneak into Nation of Islam meetings through the

THE NATION OF ISLAM

Muhammad Ali (center) applauded a speech by Nation of Islam leader Elijah Muhammad in Chicago.

Islam developed in what is now Saudi Arabia more than 1,400 years ago. The form of Islam that Muhammad Ali began practicing had been adopted by the Nation of Islam. The organization, also known as the Black Muslims, promoted black nationalism. Its leader for many years was Elijah Muhammad, who was born Elijah Poole in 1897. Poole became an assistant to W.D. Fard, the Nation of Islam's founder, in about 1930 and took over in 1934 when Fard disappeared. Elijah Muhammad said he was a messenger of Allah, the Islamic name for God. He taught that white people were devils and that Allah was a black man who had created the universe.

Elijah Muhammad's teachings mentioned a spaceship and evil scientists. But he also told blacks they should build their own businesses and take care of themselves. They could never count on whites to help them, he said. A split between Elijah Muhammad and Malcolm X developed over what the Nation of Islam should stand for. After visiting Africa and the Middle East, Malcolm X saw that people of all races could be good Muslims. He could no longer support Elijah Muhammad's teachings. Yet he still believed that most white Americans mistreated blacks.

back door. I didn't want people to know I was there.
I was afraid, if they knew, I wouldn't be allowed to
fight for the title." By the time of his first fight with
Liston, however, people knew about his involvement
with the Nation. Just weeks before the fight, Cassius
Clay Sr. told a reporter that his son had become a
Black Muslim. The fight's promoters didn't want the
word to spread, since Clay was supposed to be the
"good" African-American this time against Liston.
Clay was spending a lot of time with Malcolm X,
who had become the focus of white suspicion of, and
hatred against, the Nation of Islam. The promoters
threatened to cancel the fight if Malcolm X did not
leave Miami, the fight's location. Malcolm agreed

to leave before the fight, but he said he would return for it. He did, and he watched Clay take the championship from Liston.

After the fight, Clay announced his name change to Muhammad Ali. He made clear he didn't hate white people. But he said, "I don't believe in forcing integration. I don't want to go where I'm not wanted. If a white man comes to my house, then he's welcome. But if he doesn't want me to come to his home, then I don't want to go. I'm not mad at the white people. If they like me, I like them."

Ali's embrace of the Nation of Islam, however, was not popular with most whites and some blacks. And leading up to the second fight with Liston, his ties to Elijah Muhammad, the group's leader, stirred some fear. Tall, strong, fierce-looking Black Muslims were usually around Ali outside the ring. Some reporters wrote that death threats had been made against Liston to force him to deliberately lose. Others said supporters of Malcolm X had threatened to kill Ali. Just three months earlier, Malcom X had been assassinated, and three Black Muslims were accused of killing him. Ali had remained loyal to Elijah Muhammad even after Malcom X split from the group. Both fighters tried to ignore all the rumors and talk of killing. Each predicted he would win by an early knockout. Of course, only one of them was right.

Chapter Three

CAPTURING THE PUNCH

With all the tension and uncertainty about the second Liston-Ali fight, the police were not taking any chances. About 70 police officers and 200 security guards were in Lewiston on May 25, 1965. As fight fans entered St. Dominic's, they were searched, with police going through bags and briefcases. But even with the security, some people managed to sneak into the arena. Sam Michael was a Lewiston businessman who had helped promote the fight. Years later his son John said anyone who had wanted to shoot Ali that night could easily have gotten inside. John Michael said a would-be killer only had to "put on a delivery uniform and carry in a case of Pepsi like half my friends did."

Just after 10:30 p.m., the bell rang to start the fight. Ali's usual style was to dance around the ring a bit, making his opponent throw punches that Ali could easily avoid. But this time, Ali charged at Liston and threw a right fist that connected. Three weeks earlier, Ali had told a reporter he had dreamed about the fight. In the dream, Ali did just what he did in Lewiston—rushed Liston and threw a right-hand punch. It was a trick he had learned from another boxer, Ali said, and "it lets the bear know right now who's in charge." Ali said the dream had predicted

Ali delivered a solid blow to Liston's chin during the famous fight.

that he would win the fight with an early knockout.

Ali circled the ring, with Liston following him, trying to land his own blows. Because he was quicker, Ali avoided most of them. After a minute had passed, Ali moved in and threw a left to Liston's stomach, followed by a solid right to his chin. People watching the fight on TV across the country and in parts of Europe heard the TV announcer say, "That was the best punch, thus far, landed by the champion." Others around the ring agreed.

Liston tried to fight back with blows to Ali's body, but the champ blocked them. Then Liston tried throwing a string of left jabs. With the last, he barely missed the left side of Ali's face and fell slightly forward. As the punch went by, Ali threw the short right-hand punch that sent Liston down.

"Get up and fight, sucker!" Ali yelled. "You're supposed to be so bad! Nobody will

Ali raised his arms in triumph after Liston went down.

believe this!" As Ali stood above the fallen challenger and demanded that he get up, John Rooney took what would become the most famous photograph of his long career.

The internationally famous photographer Henri Cartier-Bresson wrote about the "decisive moment"—the instant when a photographer presses the shutter for what turns out to be a great shot. Cartier-Bresson was known as an artist. His photos hang in museums and galleries around the world. John Rooney was not known as an artist with the camera. But he captured a decisive moment that night in Lewiston.

Rooney was a photojournalist for the Associated Press. His job was to photograph news events as they happened. Based in New York City, he took thousands of news photos over a 44-year career. Rooney joined the AP in 1930. Five years later, he was part of the team of photographers that sent out the first picture on the AP's Wirephoto service. Using telephone wires and special electronic equipment, the AP could send copies of photos in minutes to newspapers that paid for its services. Before the Wirephoto service, it could take several days for the AP to send photos to its customers, using the mail, trains, or planes.

Rooney photographed a wide range of events. He won a prize in 1944 for a picture of two fallen horses at a horse race and another two years later for covering events at the United Nations.

Rooney photographed Jackie Robinson, the first
African-American to play Major League Baseball, in
1947, during his rookie season. Several years later,
Rooney took an aerial shot of the sinking luxury
liner *Andrea Doria* off the coast of Massachusetts.
In another aerial photograph made in that era,
he captured the Statue of Liberty and the New
York skyline. After President John F. Kennedy's

assassination in November 1963, Rooney was at his burial. He took a picture showing the president's brother Bobby walking with first lady Jacqueline Kennedy, with the president's flag-covered coffin nearby.

With his sports photos, Rooney developed a reputation for his boxing shots. That night in Lewiston, he was one of many photojournalists seated around the ring. Bright lights above the ring made it easier to see Liston and Ali. In Rooney's picture, that brightness in the foreground contrasts with the mostly black background behind the taunting Ali.

The photo also shows photographers on the other side of the ring—for their purposes, the wrong side. They could not get a shot of Ali's face in that decisive moment, as Rooney did. His published shot, however, was not exactly the one he took. Rooney's original shot shows referee Walcott to the left, beginning to approach the two boxers. The photo was cropped to cut out Walcott's hands and a foot, and to eliminate some of the open space of the ring. The cropped photo emphasizes Ali staring angrily down at Liston.

Under the rules of boxing, Ali should not have been standing over Liston. He should have gone to a neutral corner as soon as Liston went down. Referee Jersey Joe Walcott tried to push Ali toward one of those two corners. At the same moment, a timekeeper at ringside started the count to determine whether Liston was knocked out. A fighter has 10 seconds to get up after going down. If he does not, the fight is over. Ali at first resisted Walcott but then went to the neutral corner.

As the seconds ticked away, Liston rolled from his back to his stomach, got up on one knee, and tried to stand. Instead, he went back down to the canvas. When he finally did get up, Walcott had no idea how long Liston had been down and seemed ready to let the fight go on. Then he heard the timekeeper say, "I counted him out. I counted him out." Walcott went over to talk to the timekeeper, and called the fighters back to resume fighting. Ali began to throw more

Under the rules of boxing, Ali should not have been standing over Liston.

Jersey Joe Walcott
guided Clay to a
neutral corner as
Liston tried to get
up from the mat.

punches. Finally Walcott signaled it was over, and
that Ali had won.

Ali's fast knockdown of Liston and what followed
angered many people in the arena. Some yelled "Fix!
Fix!"—they thought Liston had agreed before the
fight to lose. Ali began calling the knockdown punch

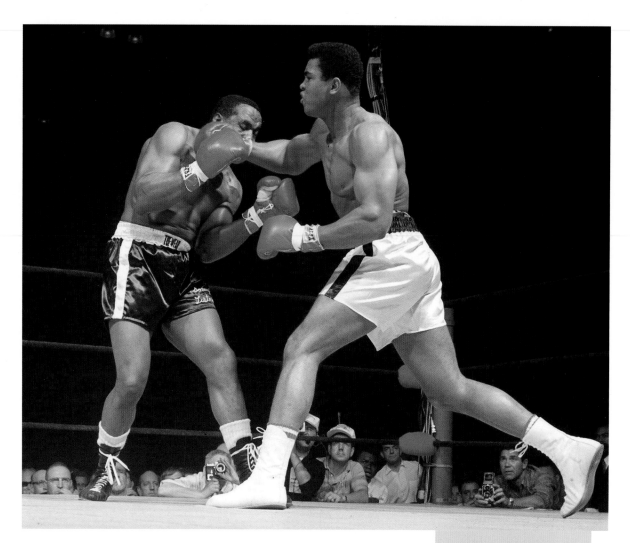

a phantom punch, meaning one his opponent could not see. But sportswriters who questioned what really happened in the ring in Lewiston called it a phantom punch for another reason. They believed the punch had never hit Liston.

The boxer José Torres was at ringside that night, covering the fight for a Spanish-language radio station. He tape-recorded what he saw as it happened: "... a perfect shot to the jaw, right on the button, and Liston is down. He's badly hurt. He might not get up."

A PHOTOGRAPHER'S TOOLS

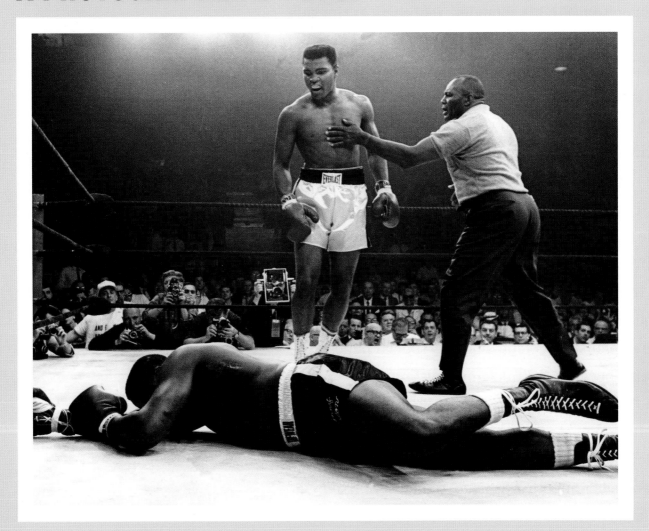

Rooney can be seen holding his camera contraption next to Ali's right knee. It appears to hold only one camera.

Unlike newspapers today, papers in 1965 rarely printed color photographs, so John Rooney shot his iconic picture using black-and-white film. But another photographer who covered the second Ali-Liston fight said he thought Rooney might have had two cameras with him that night. Neil Leifer of *Sports Illustrated* said Rooney brought a metal frame that could hold two 35 mm cameras, one on top of the other. The cameras were small and could take pictures rapidly. Using the device, said Leifer, would have let Rooney take both black-and-white and color shots. A photograph taken at the fight shows Rooney holding the metal frame, though at that point it only has one camera in it. If Rooney took color photos that night, none of them have been discovered. In 2015, though, the AP released a color photo taken almost from the same angle as Rooney's. The company doesn't know who took it. Leifer was working with color film that night, and his picture of the knockdown has become world-famous.

Torres also talked to each fighter after the bout. Ali told him that he had felt the shock of the impact with Liston's face in his shoulder. Yet others at ringside after the fight said Ali had sounded unsure about whether he had made contact. Liston told Torres, "I saw [the punch] too late." Torres later wrote that "in boxing, the punch that knocks you out is not the hard punch. It's the punch you don't see coming."

After calling his winning punch a phantom punch, Ali soon gave it a new name—the anchor punch. He said he had learned it from Stepin Fetchit, an African-American actor who said he had learned it from Jack Johnson. In 1908, Johnson became the first African-American to win the heavyweight championship. Fetchit said this special punch got its name because "it sinks anybody."

Whatever the punch was called, some people refused to believe that Ali had connected with it. The idea that the fight was fixed lingered. Today some people claim both Ali-Liston fights were fixed, but that Ali did not necessarily know they were rigged. In 2014 the *Washington Times* reported that the FBI had suspected that Liston deliberately lost the first fight to benefit mobsters betting against him. For the second fight, various stories have emerged about a fix, though no one has proven them. Recent speculation came from Paul Gallender, in his 2012 book *Sonny Liston: The Real Story behind the Ali-Liston Fights*. It quotes sources claiming that Black Muslims had threatened to

"In boxing, the punch that knocks you out is not the hard punch. It's the punch you don't see coming."

Muhammad Ali was the center of attention in New York City's Harlem neighborhood after his first-round knockout of Sonny Liston.

kill Liston's wife and son if he did not lose.

Whether either fight was fixed, two things were true after the second one. Ali, fighting under his Muslim name for the first time, was still the champion. And John Rooney had taken a great photo. The AP sent it out to newspapers around the world. Rooney won two awards for the picture: first prize in the sports category from the New York Press Photographers Association, and first prize for sports in the World Press Photo contest. Rooney continued to cover sports and other events until he retired in 1974. Ali continued to box—and stir controversy.

Chapter Four

BECOMING A LEGEND

For days after the Lewiston fight, sportswriters
continued to debate what had happened in the ring.
The ring officials had said the fight lasted one minute,
though a film of it shows that it lasted almost two
minutes. Getting something so simple so wrong made
some boxing experts question the skills of the Maine
officials who were supposed to have regulated the
fight. The film, though, also seemed to prove that
Muhammad Ali had thrown a powerful punch and hit
Sonny Liston cleanly. A slow-motion replay seemed
to confirm it. Some, however, refused to believe that
Ali had won fairly. The FBI questioned a few people
about the fight, but in the end, the U.S. attorney in
Maine decided there was not enough information to
pursue the case.

Ali defended his title only once during the rest of
1965, against Floyd Patterson. Once again Patterson
stepped into the role of the good guy, this time with
Ali as villain. Patterson even discussed the fight in
political and religious terms. He wrote in *Sports
Illustrated* that Black Muslims were a menace to
the United States and to African-Americans. "The
image of a Black Muslim as the world heavyweight
champion disgraces the sport and the nation," he
wrote. "Cassius Clay must be beaten and the Black

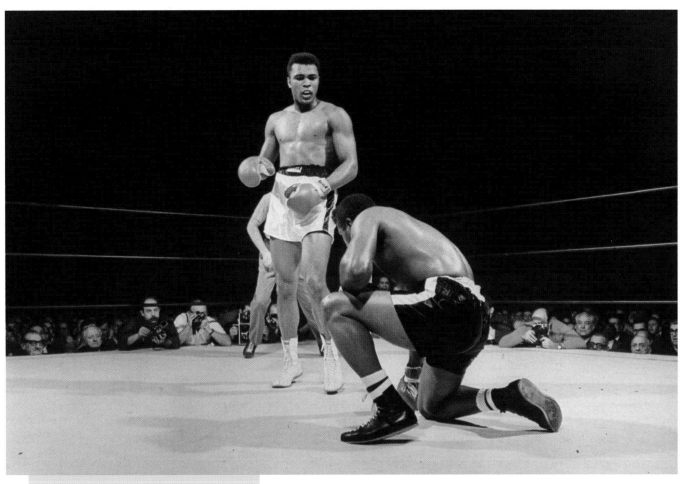

Ali (left) dominated Patterson during their 1965 heavyweight title bout in Las Vegas, Nevada.

Muslims' scourge must be removed from boxing."

Ali responded by saying he would not attack Patterson's Roman Catholic religion. "Does he think I'm going to be ignorant enough to attack his religion?" he asked. "I got so many Catholic friends of all races." He said he was an American, and he had more concern for blacks than Patterson did. Ali said that in the ring he would "punish him for the things he said; cause him pain."

During their fight, the smaller and older Patterson had no chance against Ali, who seemed to be able to hit him at will. Some people at the ring thought Ali deliberately did not knock out Patterson when he could, just so he could "cause him pain." Ali won by a technical knockout in the 12th round.

In 1966 Ali declared he did not want to get involved in the country's war with North Vietnam. Since the 1950s U.S. military advisers had been helping the South Vietnamese battle communist rebels backed by North Vietnam. The rebels were called the Viet Cong. U.S. ground troops went to Vietnam for the first time in 1965, and the country was using a draft to get more soldiers. Young men who met certain requirements would have to join the military whether they wanted to or not.

When he turned 18 in 1960, Ali had signed up for the draft, as was required by law. Four years later he had to take a physical exam and mental tests to see whether he was qualified to serve. He scored poorly on the mental tests and was told he was not qualified for the military. By 1966, though, with the demand for soldiers growing, the U.S. government had changed its rules. Ali's scores were then high enough for him to be drafted.

News reporters pressed Ali to say how he would respond if drafted. He said he knew nothing about the Vietnam War and he didn't want to fight there. "Man," he said, "I ain't got no quarrel with them Viet Cong." With that one sentence, the hatred some

Ali paused on the steps of the Louisville Veterans Adminstration office. His stance against the draft would hurt his boxing career.

whites had for Ali exploded. The war at that time was popular with many Americans. They believed government leaders when they said it was necessary for young Americans to fight communists in Vietnam. Ali, to them, seemed unpatriotic. A few people who opposed the war welcomed his refusal to fight, but most people seemed to agree with U.S. Representative Frank Clark of Pennsylvania. He said Ali was "a complete and total disgrace" for wanting to avoid military service, and he urged boxing fans to stay away from Ali's fights.

Ali met with civil rights leader Martin Luther King Jr. during his legal battle. King often spoke against the draft.

In March 1966 Ali began the legal process of challenging his being drafted. He argued that fighting in Vietnam would violate his religious beliefs. The government rejected his claim. Through 1966, Ali continued to defend his heavyweight title. *Ring Magazine*, the best-known boxing magazine, did not pick a fighter of the year for 1966. The magazine had done so for more than 30 years. It said Ali was "not to be held up as an example to the youngsters of the United States." Ali responded by saying, "You can't be loved by everybody. But I'm surprised this could

> "When are we going to wake up as a people and end the lie that white is better than black?"

happen in this country, a country with freedom of religion and belief where we go and fight in other countries for other people's freedom."

In March 1967, Ali learned he would have to report for military service. Now Ali saw his refusal as political as well as religious. He could not see why he should go to Vietnam and kill "brown people" while "so-called Negro people in Louisville are treated like dogs." Ali showed up at the building in Houston, Texas, where draftees began their military service, but he refused to be inducted. Soon he was stripped of his title and was convicted of breaking the law for his refusal to serve.

He remained out of prison while his lawyers appealed the case. But he could no longer earn a living as a boxer. No states would let him fight, and the U.S. government had taken away his passport, so he could not fight overseas. Ali began earning money giving lectures. He traveled across the United States and talked about why he opposed the war and his views on relations between blacks and whites. In one speech he asked, "When are we going to wake up as a people and end the lie that white is better than black?"

Ali went almost four years without fighting professionally. During that time, though, many people came to admire him for sticking to his principles, even if it meant going to prison. And a growing number of Americans opposed the Vietnam War, which the nation was no closer to winning than it had been in 1966. Ali won his legal battle in 1971. The U.S. Supreme Court ruled that the government should not have tried to force Ali into the military, given his religious beliefs against war.

By that time, Ali had returned to the ring. In October 1970, the city of Atlanta welcomed him to fight—Georgia did not have a state boxing commission that could prevent a bout. By then, Ali was less of a villain to many Americans, and boxing fans were eager to see whether he could regain his championship. He won the first fight and one more before facing Joe Frazier for the heavyweight title in March 1971. Frazier gave Ali his first loss as a pro. The fight, though, was considered a classic, and it began a rivalry with Frazier that lasted several years. Finally, in 1974, Ali beat George Foreman for the championship. Ali later lost the title again and regained it. After winning it in 1978 from Leon Spinks, Ali said he was retiring. But he could not stay away from the ring. "He loved boxing," said Ali's trainer, Angelo Dundee. "The gym, the competition. It was in his blood, and win or lose, he loved it to the end."

Ali announced in 1980 that he would fight again. He wanted to win the championship one more time. But by then, Ali didn't "float like a butterfly." Ferdie Pacheco, Ali's former doctor, opposed the decision. He thought Ali's body had taken too much abuse over the years. People had also begun to notice that Ali had

SEE IT *LIVE* ON BIG SCREEN CLOSED CIRCUIT TV

SUPER FIGHT II

JOE FRAZIER

MUHAMMAD ALI

NO HOME TV

NO RADIO

12 ROUNDS MONDAY JAN.28

DIRECT FROM MADISON SQUARE GARDEN

Ali won the second of three fights against rival Joe Frazier. He would win again in 1975 in what was billed the Thrilla in Manila.

trouble speaking. He went on to lose two fights and then retired for good.

As Ali showed signs that something was wrong with his health, some people said it was the result of being hit too often over a long career. Then, in 1984, he was diagnosed with Parkinson's disease. As his disease worsened, Ali rarely spoke in public, though he did make public appearances and helped raise money for Parkinson's research. He also continued to deepen his Muslim faith, though he no longer followed the teachings of the Nation of Islam.

Perhaps Ali's most emotional appearance after leaving boxing came at the 1996 Summer Olympics in Atlanta. He carried the torch that lit the Olympic flame to start the games. The games' organizers kept Ali's role a secret, and the crowd roared when it realized "the Greatest" was taking part in the event. NBC televised the ceremony. The network's Dick Ebersol had to convince Atlanta Olympic organizers that Ali deserved the honor. Some people were still critical of him because he had avoided the draft. But Ebersol pointed out that Ali was loved across the third world, including Muslim nations. Even more, he said, "Muhammad Ali may be, outside of perhaps the pope, the most beloved figure in the world."

That love poured out in 2016, when Muhammad Ali died at the age of 74. In his final hours, his wife Lonnie and his children gathered around his hospital bed in Scottsdale, Arizona. When he died, the news spread quickly around the world. Celebrities, government leaders, and sports fans paid their respects. President Barack Obama kept a pair of Ali's old boxing gloves in his private office at the White House, along with a photo of the champ. The president said Ali's willingness to fight for his beliefs

Ali stunned the world when he lit the Olympic flame at the 1996 Olympics in Atlanta.

PARKINSON'S DISEASE

Lonnie Ali stood by her husband when President George W. Bush awarded Ali the Presidential Medal of Freedom. Ali was suffering the effects of Parkinson's when he received the award in 2005.

Parkinson's disease is a progressive disease—for most people, it gets worse over time. The disease affects a part of the brain that controls speech and movement. Medication can control some symptoms for some people, but it still can't be cured. Common symptoms include shaking of the hands, called tremors, slow movements, stiffness in parts of the body, and loss of balance. People with Parkinson's might also freeze while moving and lose the ability to show a wide range of facial expressions. Scientists think Parkinson's can be caused by chemicals in the environment or by defects in genes—the chemicals that control a person's traits and how the body functions.

Looking back, people who knew Muhammad Ali well think he might have had symptoms of Parkinsonism while he was still boxing. That term refers to several movement disorders, including Parkinson's. In 1997 Ali helped start a medical center in Phoenix, Arizona, that treats Parkinson's patients; the center is named for him.

and the rights of African-Americans "helped us get used to the America we recognize today."

Years before, Ali had described how he would like to be remembered. Among other things, he hoped the world would see him as "a man who stood up for his

THE GREATEST

RACISM, WAR, MUSLIM AND AFRICAN-AMERICAN STEREOTYPES, IGNORANCE ABOUT PARKINSON'S DISEASE AND SO MUCH MORE...

MUHAMMAD ALI 1942-2016

©2016 PITTSBURGH POST-GAZETTE

An editorial cartoon based on the famous photo expressed the thoughts of many when Ali died in 2016.

beliefs no matter what" and as "a man who tried to unite all humankind through faith and love."

Even Floyd Patterson eventually saw how important a figure Ali had become. He had entertained people. He had excelled at his sport. He had risked imprisonment rather than compromise on his values. He had fought Parkinson's with dignity. "I came to love Ali," Patterson said. "I came to see that I was a fighter and he was history."

After Ali's death, both John Rooney's and Neil Leifer's photos of Ali's knockout of Sonny Liston often appeared in the media. They reminded the world of what Ali had been like in his prime. Most sports experts and photographers now say Leifer's color shot

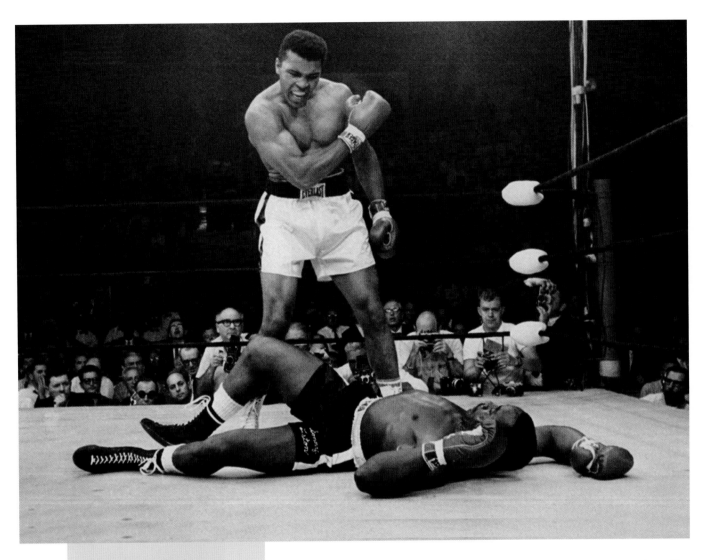

More than 50 years after it was taken, the photograph of the young, brash boxer remains one of the best sports photos ever.

of the scene is the better picture. It has greater detail, and the camera that Leifer used took a square picture with Ali perfectly centered in the frame. Leifer has spoken many times about his shot and how he took it. Rooney left no known interviews about his picture. But in the hours after the fight, it was Rooney's shot that showed Muhammad Ali as the handsome, talented, and determined boxer who later became a hero to many around the world. It remains one of the best photos ever taken of a historic American figure.

Timeline

1942

Cassius Marcellus Clay Jr. is born January 17 in Louisville, Kentucky

1954

Clay joins a gym and begins boxing; he goes on to win many amateur boxing championships

1964

Clay defeats Sonny Liston to become heavyweight world champion and then announces he has joined the Nation of Islam and wants to be called Muhammad Ali; the U.S. government rules that Ali is not eligible for the draft

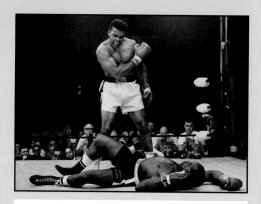

1965

During a rematch, Ali knocks out Sonny Liston in the first round; John Rooney photographs Ali challenging Liston to get up and fight; some people believe the fight was fixed

1960

Clay wins a gold medal for boxing at the 1960 Rome Olympics and then becomes a professional boxer

1962

Clay becomes friends with Malcolm X of the Nation of Islam

1967

Ali refuses induction into the U.S. Army and is found guilty of draft evasion; he begins an appeal process and remains out of prison; he is stripped of his championship and barred from boxing

1966

The U.S. government rules that Ali is eligible for the draft, and he vows not to enter the military

Timeline

1970

Ali fights for the first time since 1967 and wins two bouts

1971

Ali loses a fight with Joe Frazier, the first loss in his career; he goes on to win two fights against Frazier; the U.S. Supreme Court rules in Ali's favor and says the government denied Ali his rights when it tried to force him into the military

1996

Ali lights the Olympic flame at the Summer Games in Atlanta

1997

Ali helps found a Phoenix, Arizona, medical center that bears his name

1974

Ali regains the world championship by defeating George Foreman

1981

Ali retires with a professional record of 56 wins and five losses

1984

Ali is diagnosed with Parkinson's disease, which affects his speech and movements

2005

Ali is awarded the Presidential Medal of Freedom, the highest civilian honor

2016

Ali dies June 3 in Scottsdale, Arizona; he was 74

Glossary

civil rights—basic legal rights, such as voting, freedom of speech and religion, and equal treatment under the law

draft—system for choosing people who are forced by law to serve in the military

integration—the practice of including people of all races in schools and other public places

lynching—putting to death, often by hanging, by mob action and without legal authority

mobster—member of an organized group of criminals

neutral corner—either of the two corners in a boxing ring not used by boxers between rounds

photojournalism—use of photography to capture events and persons in the news

prejudice—hatred or unfair treatment of people who belong to a certain social group, such as a race or religion

promoters—people who finance or organize sporting events, such as boxing matches

segregation—the act of separating people in schools and other public places based on their race

spar—to practice boxing

split decision—boxing victory in which the referee and judges do not all agree on who won

technical knockout—victory in a boxing match that happens when the referee decides a fighter is too injured to keep fighting; the opponent is declared the winner

Additional Resources

Further Reading

Denenberg, Barry. *Ali: An American Champion.*
New York: Simon & Schuster Books for Young
Readers, 2014.

Killcoyne, Hope Lourie, ed. *The Civil Rights Era.*
New York: Britannica Educational Publishing/Rosen
Educational Services, 2016.

Rice, Earle, Jr. *The Vietnam War.*
Philadelphia: Mason Crest, 2015.

Internet Sites

Use FactHound to find Internet sites related
to this book. All of the sites on FactHound
have been researched by our staff.

Here's all you do:
Visit *www.facthound.com*
Type in this code: 9780756555276

Critical Thinking Using the Common Core

Why did Muhammad Ali call the punch he threw in his second fight with Sonny Liston a phantom punch? Why did others give it that name for a different reason? (Key Ideas and Details)

How did white promoters and managers sometimes treat black boxers unfairly? Do you think this still happens today? (Integration of Knowledge and Ideas)

What was the reaction among many whites when Cassius Clay changed his name and joined the Nation of Islam? What would be the reaction today to a similar action by a famous sports figure? (Craft and Structure)

Source Notes

Page 4, line 3: Sean Gregory. "Why Muhammad Ali Matters to Everyone." *Time*. 4 June 2016. 18 Oct. 2016. http://time.com/3646214/muhammad-ali-dead-obituary/

Page 4, line 20: Ibid.

Page 6, line 6: José Torres and Bert Randolph Sugar. *Sting Like a Bee: The Muhammad Ali Story*. Chicago: Contemporary Books, 2002, p. 138.

Page 6, line 24: Ibid., p. 158.

Page 7, line 6: David Remnick. *King of the World: Muhammad Ali and the Rise of an American Hero*. New York: Random House, 1998, p. 149.

Page 9, col. 1, line 9: Ibid., p. 120.

Page 9, col. 2, line 4: Ibid.

Page 10, line 4: *Sting Like a Bee: The Muhammad Ali Story*, p. 132.

Page 10, line 8: Gordon Marino. "Clay-Liston: The Fight That Made Muhammad Ali." *The Wall Street Journal*. 24 Feb. 2014. 1 Aug. 2016. http://www.wsj.com/news/articles/SB10001424052702304834704579403070448222920

Page 10, line 18: "The Fight That Launched A Champ In The Nervous Hours Leading Up To The Bout Between Cassius Clay And Heavyweight Champion Sonny Liston, The Challenger's Rap-And-Rave Antics Became The Stuff Of Sports Legend." *New York Daily News*. 6 Dec. 1998. 22 July 2016. http://www.nydailynews.com/archives/money/fight-launched-champ-nervous-hours-leading-bout-cassius-clay-heavyweight-champion-sonny-liston-challenger-rap-and-rave-antics-stuff-sports-legend--article-1.816387

Page 10, line 22: *King of the World: Muhammad Ali and the Rise of an American Hero*, p. 187.

Page 11, line 10: "Muhammad Ali: In His Own Words." CBS News. 5 June 2016. 18 Oct. 2016. http://www.cbsnews.com/news/muhammad-ali-in-his-own-words/

Page 13, line 15: *King of the World: Muhammad Ali and the Rise of an American Hero*, p. 210.

Page 14, line 2: Ibid.

Page 17, line 4: *Sting Like a Bee: The Muhammad Ali Story*, p. 78.

Page 17, line 8: Ibid.

Page 18, line 6: Ira Berkow. "Joe Elsby Martin, 80, Muhammad Ali's First Boxing Teacher." *The New York Times*. 17 Sept. 1996. 1 Aug. 2016. http://www.nytimes.com/1996/09/17/sports/joe-elsby-martin-80-muhammad-ali-s-first-boxing-teacher.html

Page 18, line 19: *Sting Like a Bee: The Muhammad Ali Story*, p. 77.

Page 19, line 3: *King of the World: Muhammad Ali and the Rise of an American Hero*, p. 92.

Page 20, line 4: Ibid., p. 96.

Page 20, line 7: Thomas Hauser. *Muhammad Ali: His Life and Times*. New York: Simon & Schuser, 1991, p. 21.

Page 22, line 20: *King of the World: Muhammad Ali and the Rise of an American Hero*, p. 115.

Page 26, line 2: Frank Litsky. "Floyd Patterson, Boxing Champion, Dies at 71." *The New York Times*. 11 May 2006. 1 Aug. 2016. http://www.nytimes.com/2006/05/11/sports/othersports/11cnd-patterson.html?pagewanted=1&_r=2

Page 26, line 6: *King of the World: Muhammad Ali and the Rise of an American Hero*, p. 14.

Page 28, line 9: Randy Roberts and Johnny Smith. *Blood Brothers: The Fatal Friendship Between Muhammad Ali and Malcolm X*. New York: Basic Books, 2016, p. 106.

Page 28, line 24: Ibid., p. 65.

Page 28, line 27: *Muhammad Ali: His Life and Times*, p. 97.

Page 31, line 6: Ibid., p. 103.

Page 32, line 13: Robert Sneddon. *The Phantom Punch: The Story Behind Boxing's Most Controversial Fight*. Camden, Maine: Down East Books, 2016, p. 183.

Page 32, line 24: *King of the World: Muhammad Ali and the Rise of an American Hero*, p. 254.

Page 33, line 9: *The Phantom Punch: The Story Behind Boxing's Most Controversial Fight*, p. 192.

Page 34, line 7: Harvey Araton. "The Night the Ali-Liston Fight Came to Lewiston." *The New York Times*. 19 May 2015. 1 Aug. 2016. http://www.nytimes.com/2015/05/20/sports/the-night-the-ali-liston-fight-came-to-lewiston.html?_r=0

Page 34, line 8: *King of the World: Muhammad Ali and the Rise of an American Hero*, p. 259.

Page 38, line 26: *The Phantom Punch: The Story Behind Boxing's Most Controversial Fight*, p. 196.

Page 39, line 4: *King of the World: Muhammad Ali and the Rise of an American Hero*, p. 259.

Page 40, line 9: *Sting Like a Bee: The Muhammad Ali Story*, p. 154.

Page 42, line 6: *Muhammad Ali: His Life and Times*, p. 128.

Page 42, line 7: Ibid.

Page 42, line 16: *The Phantom Punch: The Story Behind Boxing's Most Controversial Fight*, p. 207.

Page 44, line 22: Floyd Patterson. "Cassius Clay Must Be Beaten." *Sports Illustrated*. 11 Oct. 1965, p. 80.

Page 45, line 3: *Muhammad Ali: His Life and Times*, p. 140.

Page 45, line 8: Ibid.

Page 46, line 27: Ibid., p. 145.

Page 47, line 9: Ibid., p. 147.

Page 48, line 8: Robert Lipsyte. "Clay Fails to Get Ring's Annual Award." *The New York Times*. 28 Jan. 1967, p. 31.

Page 48, line 10: Ibid.

Page 49, line 7: *Muhammad Ali: His Life and Times*, p. 167.

Page 49, line 22: Ibid., p. 188.

Page 50, line 20: Ibid., p. 399.

Page 52, line 18: Matt Bonesteel. "Muhammad Ali almost didn't light the 1996 Olympic torch." *The Washington Post*. 21 May 2015. 1 Aug. 2016. https://www.washingtonpost.com/news/early-lead/wp/2015/05/21/muhammad-ali-almost-didnt-light-the-1996-olympic-torch/

Page 53, line 1: Steve Almasy, Madison Park and Joe Sutton. "Muhammad Ali, 'The Greatest,' Dies at 74." CNN. 4 June 2016. 1 Aug. 2016. http://www.cnn.com/2016/06/03/us/muhammad-ali/

Page 53, line 5: Ibid.

Page 54, line 8: *King of the World: Muhammad Ali and the Rise of an American Hero*, p. 299.

Select Bibliography

AP Images. http://www.apimages.com/Home

Araton, Harvey. "The Night the Ali-Liston Fight Came to Lewiston." *The New York Times*. 19 May 2015. 1 Aug. 2016. http://www.nytimes.com/2015/05/20/sports/the-night-the-ali-liston-fight-came-to-lewiston.html?_r=0

Bates, Karen Grigsby. "Muhammad Ali And Malcolm X: A Broken Friendship, An Enduring Legacy." NPR Morning Edition. 25 Feb. 2016. 1 Aug. 2016. http://www.npr.org/sections/codeswitch/2016/02/25/467247668/muhammad-ali-and-malcolm-x-a-broken-friendship-an-enduring-legacy

Berkow, Ira. "Joe Elsby Martin, 80, Muhammad Ali's First Boxing Teacher." *The New York Times*. 17 Sept. 1996. 1 Aug. 2016. http://www.nytimes.com/1996/09/17/sports/joe-elsby-martin-80-muhammad-ali-s-first-boxing-teacher.html

Bonesteel, Matt. "Muhammad Ali almost didn't light the 1996 Olympic torch." *The Washington Post*. 21 May 2015. 1 Aug. 2016. https://www.washingtonpost.com/news/early-lead/wp/2015/05/21/muhammad-ali-almost-didnt-light-the-1996-olympic-torch/

"The Decisive Moment As Henri Cartier-Bresson Meant It." *Fotografia Magazine*. 1 April 2014. 1 Aug. 2016. http://fotografiamagazine.com/decisive-moment-henri-cartier-bresson/

Ezra, Michael. *Muhammad Ali: The Making of an Icon*. Philadelphia: Temple University Press, 2009.

Gallender, Paul. "'Phantom Punch'—Mystery Solved." Boxing.com. 25 May 2014. 1 Aug. 2016. http://www.boxing.com/phantom_punch_mystery_solved.html

Gesner, Tricia, of the Associated Press. Email interview. 3 May 2016.

Gregory, Sean. "Why Muhammad Ali Matters to Everyone." *Time*. 4 June 2016. 18 Oct. 2016. http://time.com/3646214/muhammad-ali-dead-obituary/

Grimsley, Will. "AP Was There: Ali-Liston Rematch." The Associated Press. 1 Aug. 2016. http://interactives.ap.org/2015/ali-liston-fight/

Harris, Aisha. "Was There Really 'Mandingo Fighting,' Like in Django Unchained?" *Slate*. 24 Dec. 2012. 1 Aug. 2016. http://www.slate.com/blogs/browbeat/2012/12/24/django_unchained_mandingo_fighting_were_any_slaves_really_forced_to_fight.html

Hauser, Thomas. *Muhammad Ali: His Life and Times*. New York: Simon & Schuser, 1991.

Lipsyte, Robert. "Clay Fails to Get Ring's Annual Award." *The New York Times*. 28 Jan. 1967, p. 31.

Litsky, Frank. "Floyd Patterson, Boxing Champion, Dies at 71." *The New York Times*. 11 May 2006. 1 Aug. 2016. http://www.nytimes.com/2006/05/11/sports/othersports/11cnd-patterson.html?pagewanted=1&_r=2

Loverro, Thom. "FBI suspected iconic 1964 Ali-Liston fight was rigged by mob." *The Washington Times*. 24 Feb. 2014. 1 Aug. 2016. http://www.washingtontimes.com/news/2014/feb/24/was-rigged-by-mob/?page=all

Marino, Gordon. "Clay-Liston: The Fight That Made Muhammad Ali." *Wall Street Journal*. 24 Feb. 2014. 1 Aug. 2016. http://www.wsj.com/news/articles/SB10001424052702304834704579403070448222920

Matthews, Wallace. "Ali's Fighting Spirit." *Neurology Now*. March/April 2006, Vol. 2 (2), pp. 10-23. 1 Aug. 2016. https://patients.aan.com/resources/neurologynow/index.cfm?event=home.showArticle&id=ovid.com%3A%2Fbib%2Fovftdb%2F01222928-200602020-00004

Mondy, Dave. "How Things Break." *Slate*. 22 May 2015. 1 Aug. 2016. http://www.slate.com/articles/sports/sports_nut/2015/05/ali_liston_50th_anniversary_the_true_story_behind_neil_leifer_s_perfect.html

Patterson, Floyd. "Cassius Clay Must Be Beaten." *Sports Illustrated*. 11 Oct. 1965.

Puma, Mike. "Liston Was Trouble in and out of Ring." ESPN Classic. 1 Aug. 2016. http://espn.go.com/classic/biography/s/Liston_Sonny.html

Remnick, David. *King of the World: Muhammad Ali and the Rise of an American Hero*. New York: Random House, 1998.

The Ring. 1 Aug. 2016. http://www.ringtv.com

Roberts, Randy, and Johnny Smith. *Blood Brothers: The Fatal Friendship Between Muhammad Ali and Malcolm X*. New York: Basic Books, 2016.

Schonauer, David. "How *Mad Men* Rewrote Sports Photo History This Week." I Like to Watch blog. 8 Sept. 2010. 1 Aug. 2016. http://thevisualculture.blogspot.com/2010/09/how-mad-men-rewrote-sports-photo.html

Sharnik, Morton. "The four who baffled Liston." *Sports Illustrated*. 10 Feb. 1964. 1 Aug. 2016. http://www.si.com/vault/1964/02/10/608210/the-four-who-baffled-liston

Sneddon, Robert. *The Phantom Punch: The Story Behind Boxing's Most Controversial Fight*. Camden, Maine: Down East Books, 2016.

Torres, José, and Bert Randolph Sugar. *Sting Like a Bee: The Muhammad Ali Story*. Chicago: Contemporary Books, 2002.

Williams, Richard. "Muhammad Ali's phantom punch has us scratching our heads 50 years on." *The Guardian*. 22 May 2015. 1 Aug. 2016. https://www.theguardian.com/sport/blog/2015/may/22/muhammad-ali-phantom-punch-sonny-liston-1965

Index

Ali, Muhammad
 birth of, 16
 championship titles, 4–5, 11, 20, 31, 49, 50
 childhood of, 16, 17–18
 civil rights movement and, 27–28
 confidence of, 10, 11–12, 27
 death of, 52
 fighting style of, 32
 health of, 50–52, 53, 54
 lecture tour, 49
 military draft and, 46–50, 52
 name, 13, 14, 31, 43
 at Olympic Games (1960), 6, 20–21
 at Olympic Games (1996), 52
 reach of, 4
 religion of, 12–14, 28, 29, 30, 31, 44–45, 52
 retirement of, 50, 51
 suspension of, 14
 taunts, 4, 7, 8, 9, 10, 20, 22
 training, 18–19, 22
Andrea Doria (luxury liner), 36
Associated Press (AP), 35, 41, 43

Black Muslims. *See* Nation of Islam.

Cannon, Jimmy, 13–14
Cartier-Bresson, Henri, 35
Clark, Frank, 47
Clay, Cassius (ancestor), 16
Clay, Cassius, Sr., 16, 30
Clay, Odessa, 16, 20
Clay, Rudy, 16

Douglass, Frederick, 27
Dundee, Angelo, 22, 50

Ebersol, Dick, 52

Fard, W.D., 29

Fetchit, Stepin, 42
Foreman, George, 50
Frazier, Joe, 50

Gallender, Paul, 42–43

Johnson, Jack, 42

Kennedy, Jacqueline, 37
Kennedy, John F., 36–37

Leifer, Neil, 41, 54–55
Liston, Charles "Sonny," 4–6, 7, 10, 11, 12, 14–15, 22, 23–25, 26–27, 30, 31, 32–35, 38–40, 42–43, 44

Marciano, Rocky, 6
Marshall, Marty, 4
Martin, Joe, 18, 19, 21
mobsters, 22, 24, 42
Muhammad, Elijah, 13, 29, 31

National Association for the Advancement of Colored People (NAACP), 28
Nation of Islam, 13–14, 28, 29, 30, 31, 42–43, 44–45, 52
New York Times (newspaper), 26

Obama, Barack, 52–53

Pacheco, Ferdie, 10, 50
Parkinson's disease, 51–52, 53, 54
Patterson, Floyd, 6, 21, 25–26, 27, 44–46, 54

Ring Magazine, 48
Robinson, Jackie, 36
Rooney, John, 35–38, 41, 43, 54, 55

slavery, 16, 27, 28

Spinks, Leon, 50
Sports Illustrated (magazine,) 41, 44

Torres, José, 6, 40, 42

U.S. Supreme Court, 50

Vietnam War, 46–47, 48, 49–50

Wagner, "Gorgeous" George Raymond, 9
Walcott, Jersey Joe, 14, 38, 39
World Boxing Association, 14

X, Malcolm, 28, 29, 30, 31

About the Author

Michael Burgan has written many books for children and young adults during his 20 years as a freelance writer. Most of his books have focused on history. Burgan has won several awards for his writing. He lives in Santa Fe, New Mexico.